Talking with Your Toddler Activity Book

Fun Exercises and Games That:
- Promote Verbalizing
- Teach New Words
- Encourage Language

Teresa Laikko, MS, CCC-SLP
and Laura Laikko, MS, CCC-SLP

Published in the United States by:
Ulysses Press
PO Box 3440
Berkeley, CA 94703
www.ulyssespress.com

ISBN: 978-1-64604-194-7
Library of Congress Control Number: 2021931511

Printed in Canada by Marquis Book Printing
10 9 8 7 6 5 4 3 2 1

Acquisitions editor: Casie Vogel
Project editor: Ashten Evans
Managing editor: Claire Chun
Editor: Renee Rutledge
Proofreader: Beret Olsen
Front cover design: Chris Cote
Cover illustrations: © Lorelyn Medina/shutterstock.com
Interior design and production: Jake Flaherty
Interior illustrations: shutterstock.com
Production assistant: Yesenia Garcia-Lopez

CONTENTS

INTRODUCTION

Welcome to the *Talking with Your Toddler Activity Book*! The worksheets and activities in this book are designed to promote language growth in a fun and interactive way. We hope you enjoy working on them with your child.

How to Use These Worksheets

Language growth often occurs when a child is engaged in fun activities with a caring communication partner. As you complete the worksheets with your child, your enthusiasm will encourage their participation and overall enjoyment of the activities. Children are more likely to want to communicate when they are having fun!

Here are some tips for success:

1. Follow your child's lead. Leaf through the book and see what catches their eye. The book is divided into seasonal activities, but you don't need to go in order. Let your child's interest be your guide.

2. Be prepared. Gather the child-safe materials that your child will need to complete the activity, such as crayons, markers, scissors, glue, tape, and other decorative materials (stickers, pompoms, yarn, glitter, etc.).

3. To begin each worksheet, read the directions to your child. See if they can repeat the directions back. (Don't worry if they can't! Help them remember each step; it's good practice.)

4. Remember, the goal of this book is to encourage your child's language growth while enjoying fun activities. Don't worry about perfection or following directions exactly. Let your child be creative and make a mess. It will give you something to talk about!

Language Tips for Working with Your Child

You can use several strategies to encourage language production. Most of them will seem like common sense to you, as you are probably already using them.

- **Modeling:** Look at the activity or picture and talk about what you see using child-friendly language. This provides an adult model that your child can hear and learn from. For example, with our activity making a pretend pizza, you can say, "Let's make a pizza! It looks so delicious!"

- **Wait Time:** Give your child time to think and formulate a response or make a comment. Children often require longer wait times to process language and produce their own sentences. Take your time.

- **Expand:** After your child makes a comment, repeat what they say and expand on it. A good rule of thumb is to add one or two words to your child's comment. For example, if your child says "pumpkin," you can say "orange pumpkin!" or "pumpkin is big!" You don't need to do this every time your child speaks, but an occasional expansion provides your child with additional vocabulary.

- **Self-Talk:** Talk about what you're doing and thinking in simple sentences. For example, "I am cutting the paper. I want to color it pink. That's my favorite color!" Hearing sentences like this will provide your child with more language examples.

- **Open-Ended Questions:** Using open-ended questions gives your child the chance to respond with more than a yes or no answer. An example of an open-ended question is "What do you like to do when it's cold outside?" If they have trouble answering an open-ended question, guide them by providing them two choices: "Do you like to go sledding or throw snowballs?"

Extension Activities

Each theme includes ideas for extension activities beyond the worksheets. Pick and choose what appeals to you, and what you think will work best with your child. Don't worry about completing every idea, as these are only suggestions. In each extension section, we'll discuss:

Core Vocabulary: This section includes words that are related to each activity. Try to use them in the conversations that come up naturally as you work together. Hearing a word multiple times will help solidify the concept in your child's mind. See if your child understands the vocabulary and concepts. For example, if your child has trouble with the concepts of big, medium, and small, use the words in other contexts, such as in relation to what you see around the house: "Look, Dad's shoes are big! Mom's shoes are medium, and your shoes are small!"

Following Directions: Use this extension activity as a way to have fun with the topic! Following directions is a good method to improve your child's understanding of a theme or concept. In this section, we often recommend playing with a completed project while practicing spatial concepts like in, on, or on top.

Conversation Topics: These are ideas to expand on the topic and encourage conversation with your child. Remember to use the language tips listed above when talking to your child. Sometimes children just don't want to talk, and that's okay too. If the conversation begins to feel more like an interrogation, feel free to take a step back. This is supposed to be fun!

Book Suggestions: Books are a fantastic way to promote language learning. The library and YouTube are excellent sources to find age-appropriate books. Be sure to preview the entire video before showing it to your child—just in case. To make reading more fun, let your child pick the book based on their interests. We include theme-based suggestions of some of our favorite books if you need ideas.

For younger children, we recommend doing "picture walks" with the book. A picture walk consists of looking through the pictures of the book and talking about what you see. Point out what the characters are doing: "The boy is running! Where do you think he's going?" If the book is too wordy for your child, go ahead and simplify. No need to read every single word—paraphrase.

- **More Activities:** These additional ways to play within the theme will help promote and solidify concepts and vocabulary presented in the worksheets. We've included some activities to get your child moving or to use imaginative play. Once again, do only what feels right for you and your child.

- **Songs and Videos:** All of our songs and videos are child-friendly and available on YouTube at the time of this writing. Watch them together and sing along. Replay the videos as much as your child wants, or until they drive you crazy! Sing the songs at other times of the day, such as while driving in the car or when getting ready for bed. Pause the video occasionally and talk about what the characters are doing (for example, "Oh no! She fell down!"). Ask your child what they think will happen next.

Important Things to Remember

While working on these activities with your child, there are several things to keep in mind.

- Set reasonable expectations. Remember that your child is still learning! Some activities include skills they are still developing. For example, fine motor skills like cutting and coloring are challenging for young children. They may require your help using child-safe scissors or holding a crayon appropriately.

- Another developing skill is speech. Young children may not be able to produce all their speech sounds. That's okay! Repeat what they say using the correct pronunciation of words. The message behind what they say is more important than how they say it. With this workbook, we are targeting the use of language and communication rather than the production of sounds.

- Imperfection and mistakes are part of learning. Be accepting of your child's attempts to complete the activities. Helping your child is okay, but let them take ownership of their work. Resist the urge to do the activities for them. Give them the opportunity to learn how to do things for themselves. Show pride in what they've achieved; focus on the successes and not the imperfections.

- Accept creative differences. Who says a tree needs to be green? A pink tree is very pretty too! Your child might decide to do something completely different, and that's okay. Talk to them about what they're doing and encourage them to follow their vision.

FALL ACTIVITIES

Autumn reminds us of falling leaves, pumpkins, apples, and cool weather. In this section, we are going to do some fun, fall-themed activities.

Make a Pizza

Directions

Let's make a pizza! Color in the pizza sauce. You can choose red for marinara, green for pesto, or any other color you want! After coloring, choose your toppings. Cut them out and paste them on your pizza! (Parents: Ask, "How does it taste? Yummy or yucky? Hot or cold?")

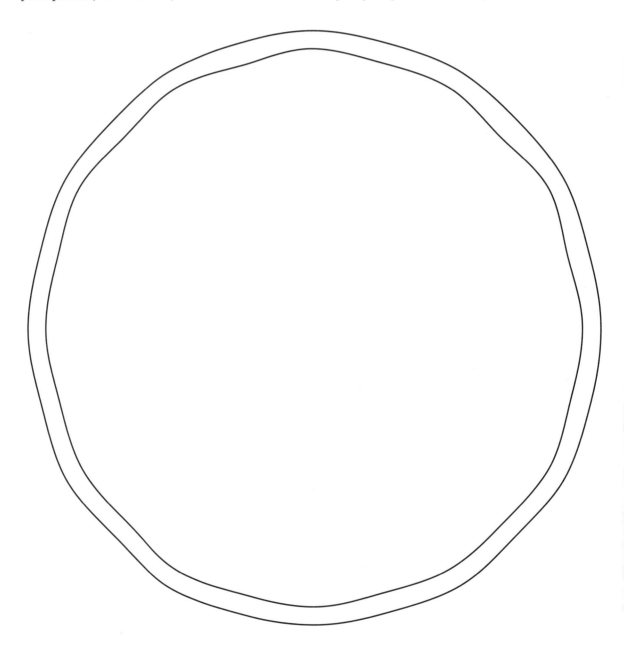

Extension Activities

Parents, here are some extension activities to promote language development with pizza play.

Core Vocabulary

- circle
- pizza
- sauce
- different toppings
- hot
- cut

- slice
- big
- medium
- small
- more
- crust

Following Directions

- Pretend to order a pizza on the phone, and ask your child to make it. Say, "I want pepperoni and cheese!" Have your child take a turn ordering pizza.

Conversation Topics

- Where do we get pizza?
- What's your favorite pizza?
- What does "delivered" mean?
- How do we order a pizza?

Book Suggestions

- *Hi, Pizza Man!* by Virginia Walter and Ponder Goembel
- *Pizza at Sally's* by Monica Wellington
- *Pizza!: An Interactive Recipe Book* by Lotta Nieminen

More Activities

- Get a blank piece of paper to draw more pizza and toppings.
- Make pizzas with any play dough. Talk about how the play dough feels soft and squishy.
- Practice rolling play dough and making pizzas of different sizes. Talk about small, medium, and large.
- Make your own little play dough toppings to put on top (they don't have to be perfect!).

🎵 "Pizza Party" by Super Simple Songs on YouTube

🎵 "I Am a Pizza" by BGSAIZ on YouTube

All about Pumpkins

Did you know pumpkins
start out as seeds?

They grow under
the ground until
they sprout!

Then they grow
yellow flowers.

Then little green
pumpkins appear.

Finally, the little green
pumpkins turn into big
orange pumpkins!

Color your own pumpkin life cycle below.

Pumpkin Patch

Directions

Look! The boy and girl grew their own pumpkins. Color and cut out the biggest pumpkin on page 19. Practice putting the pumpkin in different places. Can you put the pumpkin *on top* of the girl's head? Can you put the pumpkin *next to* the boy? Can you put the pumpkin *between* the boy and the girl? Glue it to your favorite spot and color the rest of the picture.

Extension Activities

These extension activities promote language development with pumpkin play.

Core Vocabulary

- pumpkin
- seed
- sprout
- flower
- little
- big

- orange
- pumpkin patch
- next to
- on top
- between
- round

Following Directions

- Ask your child to take their pumpkin and put it on their head. Say, "Put it behind your back. Put it under the table."
- Practice drawing a face on the pumpkin. As you do so, you can say, "First, two eyes! Next, a nose!"

Conversation Topics

- Is a pumpkin an animal or a plant?
- What do we do with pumpkins?
- Do you like pumpkin pie?
- Would you like to grow your own pumpkin?
- What would you need to grow a pumpkin? (Examples: seeds, dirt, water, sunshine.)

Book Suggestions

- *Five Little Pumpkins* illustrated by Dan Yaccarino
- *Seed, Sprout, Pumpkin, Pie* by Jill Esbaum
- *The Roll-Away Pumpkin* by Junia Wonders and Daniela Volpari
- *The Carrot Seed* by Ruth Krauss and Crockett Johnson (A carrot has a similar life cycle to a pumpkin.)

More Activities

- Draw your own pumpkins on a piece of paper. Ask your child the following questions: What color is your pumpkin? Does your pumpkin have a face? Is it happy, sad, or angry? Is your pumpkin big or little?

- Grow your own pumpkin from a seed! You can get pumpkin seeds from inside a fresh pumpkin or as ready-to-plant seeds at your local garden store. There are multiple ways to grow pumpkins—from finding a spot in your garden, to growing the seed right inside the pumpkin! Look up the best way to do it for your family. When your seed begins to sprout, use the pumpkin vocabulary to describe what you see—stems, leaves, etc. Compare the live plant with what you talked about during the activity. Ask your child questions about what they think will happen to the pumpkin plant next.

- Roast some pumpkin seeds. Find a recipe that sounds good to you—there are so many ways to spice and flavor the seeds! Talk about what they look like after they've been roasted—do they look different than before? What do they taste like?

Songs and Videos

- "Five Little Pumpkins" by Super Simple Songs on YouTube
- "Sesame Street: Making Pumpkin Faces" by Sesame Street on YouTube
- "Five Little Pumpkins Sitting on a Gate" by the Kiboomers on YouTube

Get Spooky

Here are some activities for the Halloween season. Color and cut out the pictures and put them in a bowl or a "cauldron." Pull out the pictures one by one and practice the actions you see.

Carve

Scare

Scurry

Eat

23

Flap

Cackle

Hoot

Meow

Extension Activities

Parents, here are some extension activities to promote language development with spooky Halloween play.

Core Vocabulary

- carve
- eat
- rattle
- scare
- float
- scurry
- cackle
- flap
- cauldron
- pumpkin
- jack-o'-lantern
- bat
- ghost
- witch
- skeleton
- spider
- vampire
- costume

Following Directions

- Go for a walk around your neighborhood and ask your child to count the pumpkins they see in people's yards. Ask them to mimic the happy, sad, or scary faces that you see on the jack-o'-lanterns. Example: "That pumpkin is so sad! Can you make a sad face?"

Conversation Topics

Talk about Halloween!

- What are your favorite costumes?
- What do you like about Halloween?
- What don't you like?
- Do you like scary things or not?
- What does it look like outside on Halloween?
- What do you see in the neighborhood?
- Talk about trick-or-treating and what it will look like: What will you do? What do you say?

Book Suggestions

- *Room on the Broom* by Julia Donaldson and Axel Scheffler
- *Mouse's First Halloween* by Lauren Thompson and Buket Erdogan
- *The Little Old Lady Who Was Not Afraid of Anything* by Linda D. Williams and Megan Lloyd
- *Skeleton Hiccups* by Margery Cuyler and S. D. Schindler

More Activities

- Carve a pumpkin, or make pumpkins or other Halloween creatures with play dough.
- You can draw a pumpkin on a piece of paper and take turns thinking of features to add, such as eyes, a nose, and a mouth.
- Make your own costumes with old clothes, yarn, or pillowcases. Be creative!
- Have your child paint a brown paper bag orange. Crumble up old papers and fill the bag with the paper to make it round. Tie it at the top and enjoy your new little pumpkin!

Songs and Videos

- "This Is the Way We Trick or Treat" and "Who Took the Candy?" by Super Simple Songs on YouTube
- "Five Little Pumpkins Sitting on a Gate" by the Kiboomers on YouTube
- "Sesame Street: H Is for Halloween" by Sesame Street on YouTube
- "Sesame Street: Monster in the Mirror" by Sesame Street on YouTube

Leaves

Directions

Leaves come in many different shapes and sizes. Color all the *big* leaves red and all the *small* leaves yellow.

29

Leaves on a Tree

Directions

Color the leaves and cut them out. Glue them onto the branches of the tree. Go outside and find a real leaf. Glue that onto the tree too!

Extension Activities

Parents, here are some extension activities to promote language development with leaf play.

Core Vocabulary

- leaf
- stem
- tree
- branch
- big
- small

- red
- yellow
- green
- crunchy
- rake

Following Directions

Ask your child to do the following either with the leaves from the worksheet, or with leaves you have found outside:

- Put a leaf *on top* of the tree.
- Put a leaf *under* the tree.
- Drop a leaf and see how it falls.
- Ask, "Did it fall fast or slow?"

Conversation Topics

- Do you see leaves outside?
- What color are the leaves?
- Are they big or small?
- Are they round or oval shaped?

Book Suggestions

- *We're Going on a Leaf Hunt* by Steve Metzger and Miki Sakamoto
- *There Was an Old Lady Who Swallowed Some Leaves!* by Lucille Colandro and Jared Lee

More Activities

- Go on a walk and find different leaves. Talk about their size and color: Are they crunchy if you step on them? How many did you find? Did you find a lot or just a couple?
- If you have a rake at your house, rake some leaves (or blocks or Legos) into a pile. Talk about the size of the pile: Is it big or small? Is it hard or soft?

- "Seasons Songs for Kids: Autumn Leaves Are Falling Down" by the Learning Station on YouTube
- "Why Do Leaves Change Color?" by Super Simple Songs on YouTube
- "Orange, Yellow, Red and Brown" by the Learning Station on YouTube

All about Me

Directions

Everyone's a little bit different. Let's talk about what is special about you! Look at yourself in the mirror and color in your face below.

My eyes help me see! My eyes are _____ (color). Color your eyes.

I love my hair! Is my hair curly, straight, or wavy? Draw in your hair.

Extension Activities

Parents, here are some extension activities to promote language development with play about our bodies.

Core Vocabulary

- body parts
  - eyes
  - nose
  - mouth
  - ears
  - hair
- curly
- straight
- wavy
- colors

Following Directions

- Have your child practice following one-step directions with body parts. "Touch your nose! Touch your mouth!"
- Once they are able to do that, make it more difficult by adding another step. Examples: "Touch your nose and stick out your tongue! Wiggle your ear and pat your tummy!"

Conversation Topics

- Look in the mirror with your child. Talk about what looks the same and what looks different. For example, "I have blue eyes, and you have pretty brown eyes. I love my red hair, and I love your black hair!"

Book Suggestions

- *Hair Love* by Matthew A. Cherry and Vashti Harrison
- *What I Like about Me!* by Allia Zobel Nolan and Miki Sakamoto
- *My Book about Me by Me, Myself* by Dr. Seuss and Roy McKie

More Activities

- Draw your bodies on another piece of paper.
- If you can, trace each other's bodies outside with sidewalk chalk.
- Keep your bodies healthy by practicing simple yoga. (You can find age-appropriate yoga on YouTube under "Preschool Yoga." Or, read the books *Good Morning Yoga* or *Good Night Yoga* by Mariam Gates and Sarah Jane Hinder.)

Songs and Videos

- "One Little Finger" by Super Simple Songs on YouTube
- "Sesame Street: One Fine Face" by Sesame Street on YouTube

Time for the Bus

Directions

The kids are ready to go to school! Color the picture below. Point to the girl with pigtails. Point to the boy with curly hair. Point to the boy with the backpack. Point to the girl sitting in front. Point to the boy sitting behind her.

Bus Shapes

Directions

Look for the shapes on the bus. Can you find circles? Can you find squares? Find a rectangle. Find an octagon.

38

Extension Activities

Parents, here are some extension activities to promote language development with bus play.

Core Vocabulary

- bus
- circle
- square
- rectangle
- octagon

- behind
- front
- curly
- pigtails
- backpack

Following Directions

Try the following activities with your child:

- Count the windows on the bus in the drawings.
- Cut out the bus and drive it around your house. Drive it to the bathroom. Drive it to the kitchen. Drive it *fast*, drive it *slow*, and practice *stopping*!

Conversation Topics

- What color is a school bus?
- Have you been on a bus?
- What was it like?

Book Suggestions

- *Don't Let the Pigeon Drive The Bus!* by Mo Willems
- *The Little School Bus* by Margery Cuyler and Bob Kolar

More Activities

- Set up a few chairs to re-create a bus. Have a "driver" sit up front, and "passengers" behind them. Let the driver pretend to drive the bus!
- Sing "Wheels on the Bus" or ask to go to your favorite places, such as Grandma's house, the library, or the park.

Songs and Videos

- Multiple versions of "Wheels on the Bus" are available on YouTube. Pick one of those and sing along.

Apples

Look at all these apples! Count the apples in each box and circle the correct number.

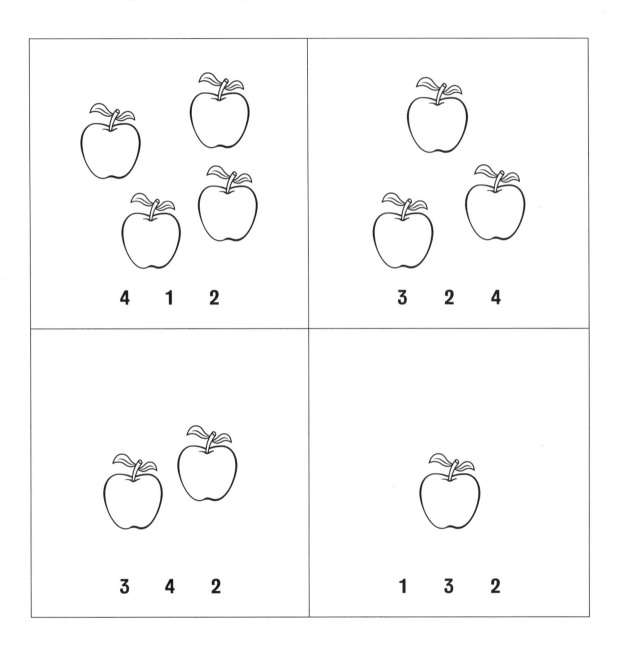

4	1	2
3	2	4
3	4	2
1	3	2

Apple Patterns

Directions

Look at the patterns. Cut out the pictures at the bottom of this page to complete the patterns. When you're finished, you can color them! Do you want red, yellow, or green apples?

Options to cut out.

Extension Activities

Parents, here are some extension activities to promote language development with apple play.

Core Vocabulary

- apple
- apple tree
- count
- numbers 1–4
- most
- fewest
- just one

- core
- stem
- leaf
- seed
- yellow
- red
- green

Following Directions

Look at your Apples worksheet on page 40. Ask your child to do the following:

- Point to the square that has the most apples.
- Point to the square that has the fewest apples.
- Point to the square that has just one apple.

Conversation Topics

- What's your favorite apple?
- Do you like red, green, or yellow apples?
- Do you like to eat apples sliced or whole?
- Can you think of some things that we make with apples? (Examples: juice, pie, crisp, etc.)
- Talk about the different parts of an apple. (Examples: leaf, stem, seeds, peel, and core.)

Book Suggestions

- *Ten Red Apples* by Pat Hutchins
- *Ten Apples Up On Top* by Dr. Seuss (Theo. LeSieg) and Roy McKie
- *Ouch!* (sometimes called *Apple Trouble*) by Ragnhild Scamell and Michael Terry

More Activities

- Eat things made from apples, such as applesauce or apple pie.
- Cut an apple in half and look at the seeds. Have your child count how many seeds they see.
- Use apple halves to dip in paint and make stamps.

🚂 Cook your favorite apple recipe. Practice using cooking vocabulary with words like "cut," "stir," and "more."

Songs and Videos

🚂 "Way Up High in an Apple Tree" by the Learning Station on YouTube

🚂 "Apples and Bananas" by Super Simple Songs on YouTube

🚂 *"Ten Apples Up On Top* Song" in the style of Jason Mraz by vancemo on YouTube

WINTER ACTIVITIES

Snow. Cold toes and noses. Hot chocolate. Warm clothes and a fire in the fireplace. Let's talk about winter!

Build a Snowman

Directions

Color the parts of the snowman and his clothes. You can even color his buttons if you want. Cut out the three circles, the arms, the hat, and the scarf. Glue them onto a new piece of paper and make a friendly snowman.

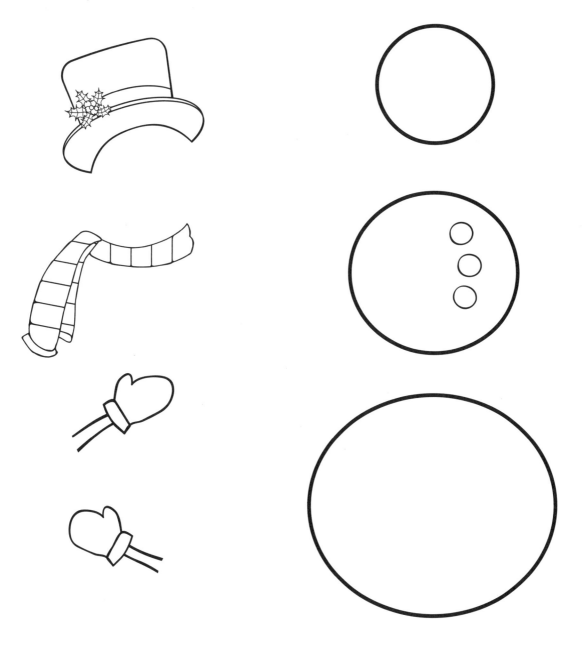

Snowman Puzzle

Directions

Color the snowman! Then cut out the strips of the puzzle on the dotted lines. Can you put your snowman back together?

Extension Activities

Parents, here are some extension activities to promote language development with snowman play.

Core Vocabulary

- snowman
- snow
- snowflake
- hat
- scarf
- buttons
- carrot
- nose
- eyes
- arms
- mouth
- cold
- sticks
- cut
- puzzle
- glue
- top
- bottom
- middle

Following Directions

- Practice the concepts *big*, *medium*, and *small*. Have your child point to the big snowball, the medium snowball, and the small snowball on the snowman they made. See if they can find other big, medium, and small things around your house.

Conversation Topics

- Have you ever made a snowman?
- Have you ever touched snow?
- What does it feel like?
- Is it hot or cold?
- Is it wet or dry?
- What do we need to make a snowman? (Examples: snow, hat, sticks, etc.)

Book Suggestions

- *Snowmen at Night* by Caralyn Buehner and Mark Buehner
- *All You Need for a Snowman* by Alice Schertle and Barbara Lavallee
- *There Was a Cold Lady Who Swallowed Some Snow!* by Lucille Colandro and Jared Lee

More Activities

- If you have cotton balls, have your child glue them onto the body of one of the snowmen they made. Talk about how they feel *soft*.
- Build your own snowman together: Fill three plastic trash bags with crumpled-up paper, newspaper, and magazines in order to make them round. Add a face with markers or shapes cut out of paper.
- Make a snowman with marshmallows. Stack three marshmallows on top of each other. Either connect them with a toothpick or with bits of frosting to keep them together. Use pretzels for the arms. With frosting, attach candies for eyes, a nose, and mouth.

Songs and Videos

- "Little Snowflake" by Super Simple Songs on YouTube
- "I'm a Little Snowman" by the Kiboomers on YouTube
- "Snow Man Freeze Song" by the Learning Station on YouTube

Hot Chocolate and Marshmallows

Directions

Yum! It is so fun to drink hot chocolate and marshmallows on a cold winter's night! Some people like a *lot* of marshmallows and some people like just a *few*.

Which mug of hot chocolate has *more* marshmallows? Which mug of hot chocolate has *fewer* marshmallows? Color the mug you like. Do you like the one with *more* or *fewer* marshmallows? If you like both, color them both!

Extension Activities

Parents, here are some extension activities to promote language development with hot chocolate and marshmallows play.

Core Vocabulary

- hot
- chocolate
- marshmallow
- more
- fewer
- mug

Following Directions

- Ask your child to touch each marshmallow in the mugs and count them. Pretend the mugs are filled with very hot chocolate. Touch the mug and say, "Ouch!" Then blow on the mugs to make the chocolate "cooler."

Conversation Topics

Talk about what the hot chocolate tastes like.

- Is it sweet or sour?
- Is it hot or cold?
- What can you do if it is too hot to drink right away?

Book Suggestions

- *Do Frogs Drink Hot Chocolate?: How Animals Keep Warm* by Etta Kaner and John Martz
- *Sneezy the Snowman* by Maureen Wright and Stephen Gilpin

More Activities

- Make hot chocolate at home. If you have marshmallows, count them as you put them in your cup.
- As a way to practice calming breaths, you can watch "Hot Chocolate" by Kira Willey on YouTube.

Songs and Videos

- "Hot Chocolate" from *The Polar Express* (available to watch on YouTube)
- "Hot Chocolate" by LoveBug & Me Music on YouTube

Bakery

Directions

Color the menu and the treats. Cut them all out. Show the menu to an adult and have them choose a treat. Then you can "sell" them their treat!

Bakery Menu

Cookie $1

Donut $2

Cupcake $3

Gingerbread Man $4

Extension Activities

Parents, here are some extension activities to promote language development with bakery play.

Core Vocabulary

- bakery
- cake
- cookies
- donut
- gingerbread man
- cupcake
- sweet
- oven
- hot
- cool
- crunchy
- crumbly
- chewy
- chocolate
- vanilla
- strawberry
- frosting
- sprinkles
- next to
- on top
- under

Following Directions

- Take turns ordering from the menu. Get out a plate and sit at the table. Ask your child to bring the treat to you. Tell them to put it next to your plate, on top of your plate, or be silly and put it under your plate!

Conversation Topics

- What is your favorite sweet treat?
- Do you like crunchy or soft treats?

Book Suggestions

- *If You Give a Mouse a Cookie* by Laura Numeroff and Felicia Bond
- *Mr. Cookie Baker* by Monica Wellington
- *Pete the Cat and the Missing Cupcakes* by Kimberly Dean and James Dean

More Activities

- Bake your favorite treat together, or use play dough to make cookies, donuts, cakes, or gingerbread men.
- Go to the bakery section of a grocery store or a coffee shop and talk about the different items. Look at the prices. Ask your child, "What numbers do you see?"

- 🚋 "Pat-a-Cake" by Super Simple Songs on YouTube
- 🚋 "The Muffin Man" by Super Simple Songs on YouTube
- 🚋 "Down at the Bakery Song" by the Kiboomers on YouTube

I Can Be Kind

Directions

Kindness shows you care about your friends and family. It can make other people feel good. Color in the pictures showing some of the ways to be kind, and then draw a picture of another way you can be kind.

Clean up toys.

Share with someone else.

Give someone a high five.

Tell someone thank you.

Invite someone to play.

What's your favorite way to be kind?

Extension Activities

Parents, here are some extension activities to promote language development with kindness-themed play.

Core Vocabulary

- kind
- kindness
- share
- invite
- help
- listen

- please
- thank you
- nice
- compliment
- take turns

Following Directions

- Practice kindness with your child. Remind them to take turns and share their toys while playing. Act out being kind with toys such as dolls or action figures. Make up scenarios for the dolls to be kind to each other. They can say things like, "Thank you for sharing! You're a good friend!"

Conversation Topics

- What does it mean to be kind?
- Has anyone been kind to you?
- Have you been kind to anyone?
- What can we do to be kind?
- If someone is feeling sad (hurt, lonely, etc.), how can we be kind?

Book Suggestions

- *The Kindness Book* by Todd Parr
- *Kindness Counts* by R. A. Strong and Ekaterina Trukhan
- *How Do Dinosaurs Play with Their Friends?* by Jane Yolen and Mark Teague
- *Strictly No Elephants* by Lisa Mantchev and Taeeun Yoo

More Activities

🚂 Make a card for a special friend or relative.

🚂 Make a kindness tree at home: Cut out a tree with empty branches from paper, as well as ten paper hearts. Whenever you see your child doing something kind, put a heart on the kindness tree. When the tree is filled with hearts, celebrate! (Don't remove hearts if the child acts up; it's just for rewarding kindness.)

Songs and Videos

🚂 "Sesame Street: Try a Little Kindness (with Tori Kelly)" by Sesame Street on YouTube

🚂 "Be Kind to Everyone (a Song about Being Kind)" by Rocking Dan Teaching Man on YouTube

Bears

Directions

Did you know that in the winter, some bears hibernate? This means they spend the winter sleeping to stay warm. Let's make a bear together. Color and cut out the bear's face.

Trace your hand on a piece of paper with your fingers pointing down. Color your hand brown or your favorite color. The palm of your hand will be the bear's body and your four fingers its paws! Glue your bear face over your thumb to cover it. What a cute bear!

Extension Activities

Parents, here are some extension activities to promote language development with bear-themed play.

Core Vocabulary

- face
- body
- legs

- paws
- trace
- hibernate

Following Directions

- Ask your child to take the bear they made during this activity and help them hibernate. Have them put their bear in bed to keep warm for winter. Wrap the bear up in a blanket and tuck them in. Sing a goodnight song or read a story to the bear together. When the bear wakes up, pretend to feed them some honey.

Conversation Topics

- What do you think a bear looks like?
- What does "hibernate" mean?
- What do you think bears dream about during the long winter?
- Where do bears live?
- Bears like to eat honey. What's your favorite food?

Book Suggestions

- *Bear Snores On* by Karma Wilson and Jane Chapman
- *Brown Bear, Brown Bear, What Do You See?* by Bill Martin Jr. and Eric Carle
- *Where's My Teddy?* by Jez Alborough
- *The Little Mouse, the Red Ripe Strawberry, and the Big Hungry Bear* by Audrey Wood and Don Wood
- *We're Going on a Bear Hunt* by Michael Rosen and Helen Oxenbury
- *Corduroy* by Don Freeman

More Activities

- Do a bear hunt: cut out or draw bear paw prints and put them around your house.
- Take a bear walk: take turns walking and growling like a bear!

🚃 "My Teddy Bear" by Super Simple Songs on YouTube

🚃 "Teddy Bear, Teddy Bear, Turn Around" by the Kiboomers on YouTube

🚃 "The Bear Went over the Mountain" by Super Simple Songs on YouTube

Snow Play

Color the images, then cut out the dice template below. Fold along the lines and glue together to make a cube. Roll the dice and take turns practicing the actions you see!

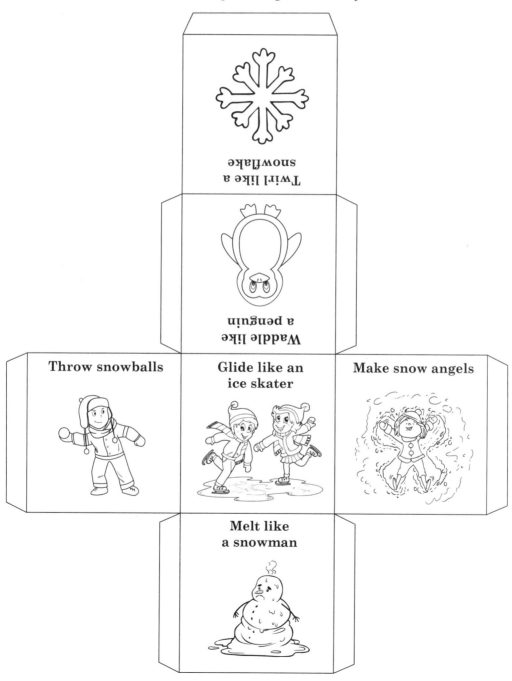

Twirl like a snowflake

Waddle like a penguin

Throw snowballs

Glide like an ice skater

Make snow angels

Melt like a snowman

Extension Activities

Parents. here are some extension activities to promote language development with snow play.

Core Vocabulary

- twirl
- waddle
- glide
- melt
- snow
- snowman
- snowflake
- cold
- penguin
- snow angel
- shiver
- shovel

Following Directions

Ask your child to roll the cube twice. Ask them the following questions:

- Can you remember what two actions to do? Can you remember three actions?
- Have your child try doing the actions in slow motion, and then try doing them really fast.

Conversation Topics

- What do you like to do when it's cold outside?
- What are some of your favorite winter-themed movies?

Book Suggestions

- *Snowmen at Night* by Caralyn Buehner and Mark Buehner
- *The Snowy Day* by Ezra Jack Keats
- *Winter Is Here*: by Kevin Henkes and Laura Dronzek

More Activities

- Think of more winter actions to do. Take turns thinking of new actions and seeing how silly you can be! How about "shoveling snow" or "putting on your hat or boots"?
- On YouTube, look up videos of people playing in the snow. Talk about what they are doing.

Songs and Videos

- "Snowflakes: Winter Action Song for Kids" by Intellidance on YouTube
- "Snow Man Freeze Song" by the Learning Station on YouTube

SPRING ACTIVITIES

Spring makes us think of flowers, sweet smells, and green grass. In this section, we will celebrate all things spring.

I Can Hike

Let's go on a scavenger hunt! Go on a walk or a hike and look for the items from the list. When you spot an item, check it off the list. If you're able to, bring some of the smaller items home with you, such as a small rock, a pretty flower, or a leaf!

Scavenger hunt/nature walk activity:

❑ Leaf

❑ Flower

❑ Rock

❑ Spiderweb

❑ Bird

❑ Butterfly

❑ Bug

❑ Cloud

❑ Grass

❑ Stick

Extension Activities

Parents, here are some extension activities to promote language development with hiking play.

Core Vocabulary

- hike
- walk
- nature
- bug
- tree

- stick
- grass
- tree
- clouds

Following Directions

- Place the items your brought home with you in order from smallest to biggest. Now, ask your child to try to put them in order from lightest to heaviest. Take an object you found on your walk and put it on a blank piece of paper. Ask your child to trace around the object using a crayon or marker.

Conversation Topics

Talk about what you think you're going to see on your nature walk before you go.

- Do you think it will be hot or cold outside?
- Will you see the sun or the moon in the sky?
- After your walk, talk about what you did see: What was your favorite part?

Book Suggestions

- *We Walk Through the Forest* by Lisa Ferland and Yana Popova
- *The Hike* by Alison Ferrell
- *Do Princesses Wear Hiking Boots?* by Carmela LaVigna Coyle, Mike Gordon, and Carl Gordon
- *Nature's Wonders* by Alejandro Algarra and Gustavo Mazali

More Activities

- Help your child press some of the items you found on the scavenger hunt into play dough.
- See if the item made an impression. Ask, "What does it look like? What does it feel like?"
- Get a container of water or use the sink. Say, "Guess which items will sink and which items will float. Were you right?"
- Help your child make a collage of some of the items you found. Glue them onto a piece of sturdy paper or cardboard.

🚂 Show your family what you found.

🚂 Play a guessing game while you are outside. Start with "I spy something (name a color or attribute)" and take turns guessing what has been spied.

Songs and Videos

🚂 "Walking in the Forest" by Super Simple Songs on YouTube

🚂 "Sesame Street: Nature Walk" by Sesame Street on YouTube

🚂 "Sesame Street: Exploring Outdoors" by Sesame Street on YouTube

Rain, Rain

We love to play in the rain! Color the picture in this order:

1. What is behind the clouds? Color that first.

2. Who is holding an umbrella above the head? Color this child next.

3. Which child is in the middle? Now color this child.

4. What is growing on the ground? Color that last.

Extension Activities

Parents, here are some extension activities to promote language development with rain play.

Core Vocabulary

- sun
- rainbow
- clouds
- rain
- splash
- umbrella
- behind
- above
- middle
- on
- wet
- first
- next
- last
- melt

Following Directions

- With the previous drawing, practice the concepts (first, next, last) you just learned. For example, you can say: "First, point to a child, *next* point to the sun. Point to the umbrella *last.*"

Conversation Topics

- Do you like rainy days?
- What can we do when it rains?
- How does the sound of rain make you feel?

Book Suggestions

- *Raindrop, Plop!* by Wendy Cheyette Lewison and Pam Paparone
- *The Big Umbrella* by Amy June Bates and Juniper Bates

More Activities

- Take a paintbrush and a cup of water. Go outside and have your child "paint" with the water on the sidewalk. They can paint letters, shapes, and numbers.
- Take an ice cube outside on a sunny day. Check the ice cube throughout the day. Ask your child to tell you what is happening to the ice cube. Is it getting bigger or smaller? Talk about the words "melting" and "wet."

Songs and Videos

- "Rain, Rain, Go Away" by Super Simple Songs on YouTube
- "The Eensy Weensy Spider" by Super Simple Songs on YouTube

Colors of the Rainbow

Sometimes, when it rains outside, we can see a rainbow in the sky. A rainbow is made of many colors. Fill in the different colors of the rainbow below. You can glue cotton balls or cut-up bits of paper onto the clouds to make them fluffy.

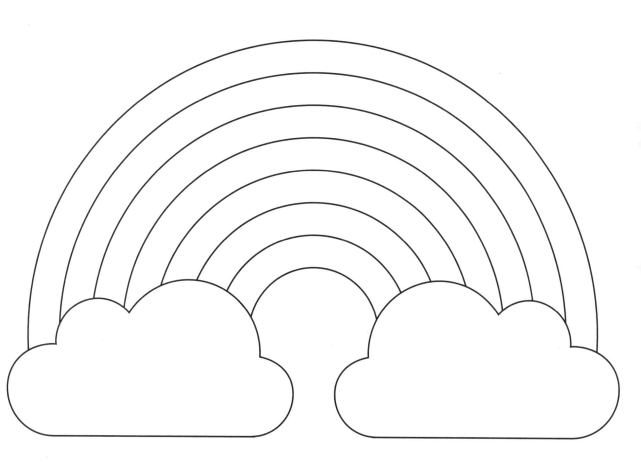

79

Extension Activities

Parents, here are some extension activities to promote language development with rainbow play.

Core Vocabulary

- rainbow
- red
- orange
- yellow
- green
- blue
- indigo
- violet
- rain
- clouds
- top
- middle
- bottom

Following Directions

- Ask your child to point to the color that is at the top of the rainbow. Next, have them point to the color that is at the bottom of the rainbow. Finally, have them point to some colors that are in the middle of the rainbow.

Conversation Topics

- Ask your child what colors they see in the rainbow. Ask them what their favorite color is. Talk about items that are a certain color. For example, "What are some things that are blue? I can think of the sky, your blue shirt, etc."

Book Suggestions

- *Rainbow: A Book of Colors* by Jane Cabrera
- *Bear Sees Colors* by Karma Wilson and Jane Chapman

More Activities

- Go on a rainbow toy hunt: look for a toy for each color of the rainbow, such as a *red* fire truck, an *orange* ball, and so on.
- You can roll out different colors of play dough and have your child place them in the lines of the rainbow outline on page 79.

- "Rainbow Song" by Super Simple Songs on YouTube
- "Rainbow" by Nancy Kopman
- "Somewhere Over the Rainbow" by Israel Kamakawiwo'ole on lgflower on YouTube (features pictures of real rainbows set to the beautiful song)
- "The Rainbow Colors Song" by A. J. Jenkins for KidsTV123 on YouTube

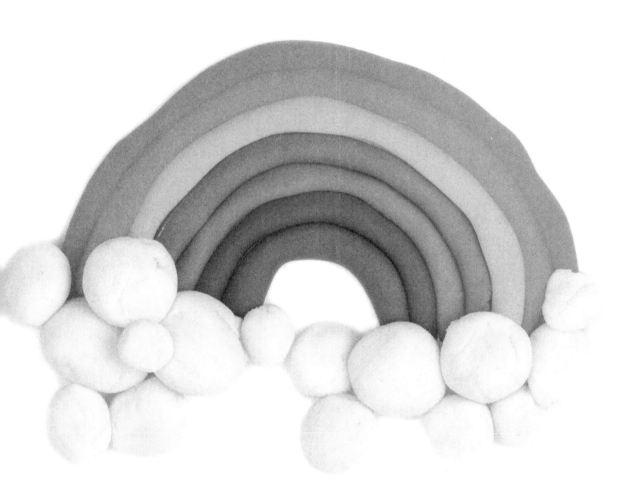

Ladybug

Color the picture. Find the ladybug with the *most* spots! Find the ladybug with just *one* spot! Who has *more* spots?

Honey Bees

Directions

Color the beehive below and the bees on page 85. Cut out the bees. You can tape each of the bees to each one of your fingers, and fly the bees around! Fly them *fast*, fly them *slow*, and fly them *up* and *down*. After you're finished flying with the bees, glue them onto the beehive so they can collect honey.

Extension Activities

Parents, here are some extension activities to promote language development with play around the themes of ladybugs and bees.

Core Vocabulary

- ladybug
- bee
- honey
- spots
- hive
- bugs
- insects
- fly

- buzz
- up
- down
- fast
- slow
- body parts
- ouch

Following Directions

- Take turns pretending the ladybug or bee landed on different body parts. Say, "Point to your head! Point to your nose!"

Conversation Topics

- How are a ladybug and a bee the same?
- How are they different?
- Which bug do you like better, and why?

Book Suggestions

- *The Grouchy Ladybug* by Eric Carle
- *I Am a Bee: A Book about Bees for Kids* by Rebecca McDonald and James McDonald

More Activities

- Play bumblebee with the little bee cutouts above. Fly the bees around and "sting" each other. Say "ouch!"
- Look up pictures of real ladybugs and bees. Talk about what they look like, what colors they are, and if they are cute or scary. Ask, "Are you afraid of them?"

- "Children's Song: I'm Bringing Home a Baby Bumblebee" by Miss Nina on YouTube

- "Here Is the Beehive" by Super Simple Songs on YouTube

- "Frank Leto's Ladybug Ladybug Song" by Montessori Home on YouTube (This is a good song to talk about body parts!)

- "Sesame Street: Ladybug's Picnic" by Sesame Street on YouTube

Bunny Hop

Bunnies love to hop! Color each of the bunnies a different color. Cut the bunnies out and put them on the floor. Hop from one bunny to the next! See how fast and slow you can go. You can also have an adult write a number on each bunny. Then, practice hopping that many times.

Bunny Hat

Cut out the outline of the bunny ears on page 93. Have an adult help you add a strip of paper about 2 inches high to make it fit around your head—overlap the strip a bit to give you space to connect the headband. If you'd like, draw the bunny's face in the middle of the strip. Staple the headband. Glue or tape the bunny ears above the bunny face on the inside of the headband. This is what it will look like:

Pretend you are a bunny and hop around. Eat a carrot!

If you drew a face on your bunny hat, practice identifying body parts. On your bunny hat, have them point to the bunny's eyes.

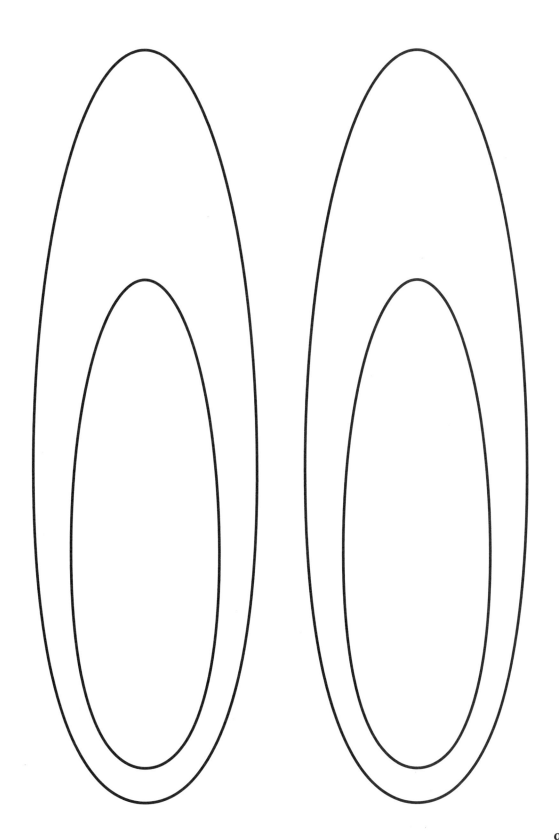

Extension Activities

Parents, here are some extension activities to promote language development with bunny play.

Core Vocabulary

- bunny
- hop
- ears
- nose
- eyes
- floppy
- rabbit
- whiskers
- numbers 1–5
- carrot
- soft

Following Directions

- Ask your child to wiggle their nose like a bunny. If you drew a face on the bunny hat (page 91), have them point to the bunny's eyes. Say, "Point to the bunny's ears. Point to the bunny's nose. Now point to your nose, ears, and eyes!"

Conversation Topics

- Bunnies love to hop! Can you think of another animal that hops?
- What do bunnies like to eat?
- What do you like to eat?
- Have you ever seen a real bunny?

Book Suggestions

- *It's Not Easy Being a Bunny* by Marilyn Sadler and Roger Bollen
- *The Runaway Bunny* by Margaret Wise Brown and Clement Hurd
- *The Velveteen Rabbit* by Margery Williams and William Nicholson

More Activities

- Look up pictures and videos of rabbits. Ask, "What do they look like? Do they look soft or rough?"
- Rabbits eat carrots, broccoli, and even some flowers. Have your child draw, color, and cut out some of these. Take turns wearing the bunny headband and pretending to eat them. If you have carrots at your house, have a real rabbit snack.

Songs and Videos

- "Sleeping Bunnies" by Little Baby Bum on YouTube
- "Five Little Bunnies Song for Kids" by the Kiboomers on YouTube

Apples and Bananas

Apples and bananas are yummy fruits. Color the apples and bananas below and the baskets on page 99. Cut out the apples and bananas. Put all the apples in one basket and all the bananas in another basket.

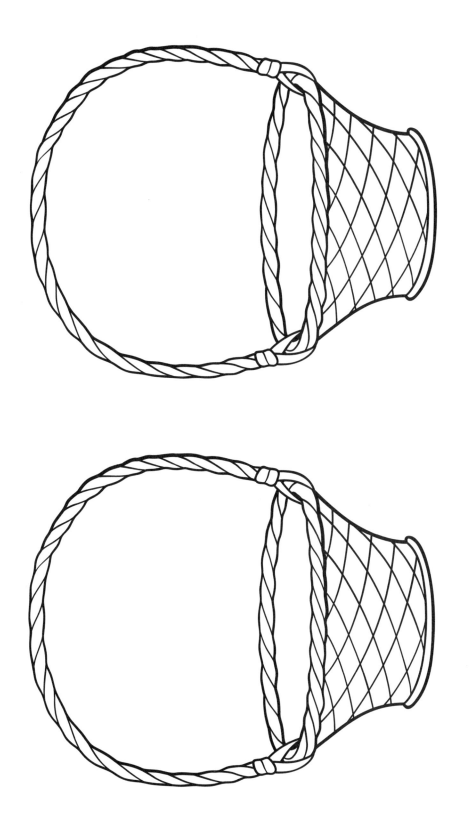

Fruit Patterns

Directions

Look at the patterns. Figure out which fruit comes next in each pattern. You can cut out the fruit at the bottom of this page and glue it in the right box, or you can just draw the correct fruit in each box.

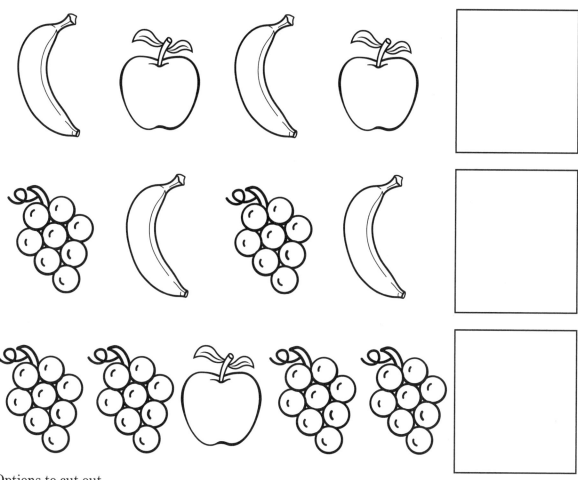

Options to cut out.

Extension Activities

Parents, here are some extension activities to promote language development with fruit play.

Core Vocabulary

- fruit
- apple
- banana
- basket
- big
- little
- strawberry

- grapes
- bunch
- sweet
- crisp
- mushy
- juicy

Following Directions

Find some fruits in your house. Try balancing a piece of fruit on your head, then ask your child to give it a try. Ask, "Can you walk across the room with it balanced on your head?" Find some smaller fruit, like berries or grapes. Count out three. Eat one. Now ask, "How many are left?"

Conversation Topics

What is your favorite fruit?

What foods can we make with apples? (Examples: apple pie, applesauce.)

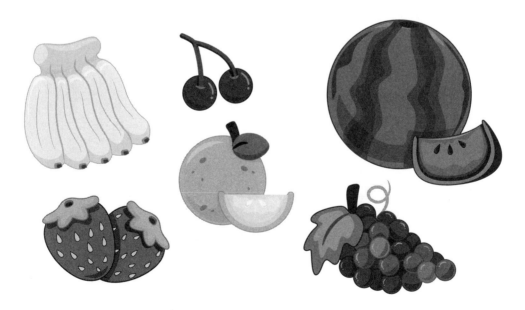

Book Suggestions

- *The Little Mouse, the Red Ripe Strawberry, and the Big Hungry Bear* by Audrey Wood and Don Wood
- *Pete the Cat and the Bad Banana* by James Dean and Kimberly Dean

More Activities

- Make faces with fruit! Find a base, such as a bagel, rice cake, or piece of toast, and have your child spread peanut butter or cream cheese on top. Add fruit toppings to make a face, such as grapes for eyes and an apple slice for a mouth. Be creative!
- Take a walk through the grocery store together and talk about your favorite fruits. Talk about what colors they are, and if they are big or small.

Songs and Videos

- "Apples and Bananas" by Super Simple Songs on YouTube

Farm Animals

Directions

Animals live in different places. Here are some animals that live on a farm. There are six farm animals and actions. Cut them out and tape or glue them to each side of a tissue box (the cube shape). Roll it on the floor and do the action that it lands on!

Flap like a chicken

Gallop like a horse

Roll like a pig

Waddle like a duck

Hop like a bunny

Chew like a cow

Extension Activities

Parents, here are some extension activities to promote language development with farm animal play.

Core Vocabulary

- farm
- farmer
- bunny
- cow
- duck
- pig
- horse
- chicken
- hop
- chew
- waddle
- roll
- gallop
- flap
- slowly
- quickly
- forward
- backward

Following Directions

- Try different ways to gallop like a horse with your child: Gallop slowly, gallop quickly. Roll, or wallow, like pigs across the room.
- Waddle like ducks. Waddle forward, waddle backward.

Conversation Topics

- Would you like to visit a farm?
- What animals would you see on a farm?

Book Suggestions

- *Mrs. Wishy-Washy's Farm* by Joy Cowley and Elizabeth Fuller
- *Click, Clack, Moo: Cows That Type* by Doreen Cronin and Betsy Lewin
- *Giggle, Giggle, Quack* by Doreen Cronin and Betsy Lewin
- *Roll Over!: A Counting Song* by Merle Peek

More Activities

🚂 Find child-friendly videos of real farm animals to watch. Talk about the animals that you see.

🚂 Visit a petting zoo. While you're there, find the biggest and smallest animals. Listen to the sounds the animals make and see if you can imitate them. Talk about how the animals feel when you touch them. Are they soft? Talk about what animals like to eat. Do humans eat the same things?

Songs and Videos

🚂 "Old MacDonald Had a Farm" by Super Simple Songs on YouTube

🚂 "The Baby Animals Song" by A. J. Jenkins for KidsTV123 on YouTube

Airplanes

Directions

In the windy spring air, airplanes can go far! Get two sheets of paper and make two paper airplanes—one for you and one for someone else. Below is an idea for how to fold your airplanes, but feel free to get creative! Color your airplanes so you know which one is which. Have a contest to see who can fly their airplane the farthest. See if you can land your plane on certain places: a table, a square drawn with chalk on the sidewalk, or on numbers written with tape or chalk.

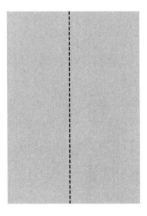

1. Fold in half the long way and lay flat.

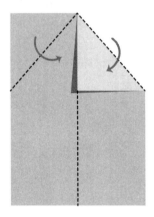

2. Take the top corners and fold in to the center line.

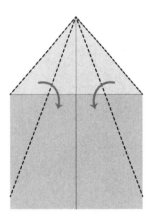

3. Fold the left and right sides to the center line again.

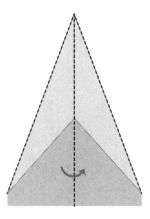

4. Fold in half on the center line.

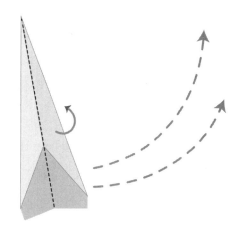

5. Take the outside flap and fold back toward the center fold.

6. Repeat on the other side.

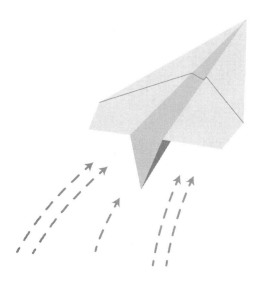

7. Your airplane is ready to fly!

Extension Activities

Parents, here are some extension activities to promote language development with airplane play.

Core Vocabulary

- airplane
- fly
- sky
- wings
- pilot

- high
- low
- fast
- slow
- flight attendant

Following Directions

Ask your child to practice following directions with spatial concepts: fly your plane *over* the chair, fly your plane *under* the table and *around* the rug. Take turns giving directions and following directions. You can ask, "Where should my plane go?"

Conversation Topics

- Would you like to go on an airplane?
- Where would you like to fly?
- Would you like to be a pilot and fly a plane?

Book Suggestions

- *Richard Scarry's A Day at the Airport* by Richard Scarry
- *The Little Airplane* by Lois Lenski
- *Planes Board Book* by Byron Barton

More Activities

- Use Google Earth on a computer or tablet. You can show your child how to click the button called "I'm Feeling Lucky" and see where in the world you "fly" to.
- Try visiting a website called WindowSwap, which allows you to look out people's windows around the world.
- Try making an airplane with craft sticks. Ask, "Do you like this one or the paper one better?"
- If you have a large cardboard box around, you can encourage your child to sit in the box and pretend it is a plane. Ask where they'd like to fly to.
- Get some cotton balls and place your airplane among "clouds."

- "Ten Little Airplanes" by Super Simple Songs on YouTube

- "Let's Be Planes" by Maple Leaf Learning on YouTube

- "Aeroplane Aeroplane Up in the Sky" by Preeti Sagar Nursery Rhymes on YouTube

SUMMER ACTIVITIES

Hot days, cold ice cream, and jumping in the pool. Let's do some fun activities all about summer!

Make an Ice Cream Sundae

Let's make an ice cream sundae. Yum! Color the bowl of ice cream. Decide which toppings you want on top. Do you want a cherry, fudge, whipped cream, sprinkles, or all of them? Color them, cut them out, and glue them on top of the ice cream.

Ice Cream Shapes

Let's talk about shapes. Look for triangles △, circles ○, rectangles ▭, and ovals ⬭. Look for the shapes in the ice cream and popsicle pictures. Color the circles pink, the triangles blue, the ovals yellow, and the rectangles green!

Extension Activities

Parents, here are some extension activities to promote language development with ice cream play.

Core Vocabulary

- ice cream
- scoop
- cone
- cup
- sprinkles
- toppings
- melt
- drip
- cold
- sticky
- chocolate
- vanilla
- strawberry
- sweet
- circle
- triangle
- rectangle
- oval

Following Directions

- Have your child practice drawing their own ice cream out of shapes. They can make a triangle cone and circles for ice cream scoops. Have your child color them in their favorite colors.
- Go on a shape hunt around your house: Together, find something that is oval, rectangular, circular, and triangular.
- Try to find cold things around your house as well. Ask, "Where can you find something cold?"

Conversation Topics

- What happens if you leave your ice cream outside on a hot day?
- What's your favorite flavor of ice cream?
- Do you like ice cream in a cone or a cup?
- How do you feel when you get ice cream?

Book Suggestions

- *Should I Share My Ice Cream?* by Mo Willems
- *The Little Ice Cream Truck* by Margery Cuyler and Bob Kolar

- Have your child pretend they own an ice cream shop. Order ice cream from them.
- Eat a bowl of real ice cream together. Ask, "Is it cold or hot? Is it sweet or sour?"
- Pretend an ice cube is a scoop of ice cream. Take it outside and see what happens.

Songs and Videos

- "The Ice Cream Song" by Super Simple Songs on YouTube
- "Shapes Song 2" by KidsTV123 on YouTube

Octopus Fun

Directions

Let's make an octopus! Cut out the octopus's body or copy the shape onto construction paper. Now cut long strips of paper for his arms. Fold the paper strips accordion style to make bendy arms (tentacles). Glue the legs onto the octopus's body and help him swim around your house.

Extension Activities

Parents, here are some extension activities to promote language development with octopus play.

Core Vocabulary

- swim
- tentacles
- ocean
- saltwater
- fish

- sand
- octopus
- under
- over
- top

Following Directions

- Ask your child to try the following activities:
- Count the octopus's arms.
- Put the octopus on top of the table.
- Put the octopus under the table.
- Make him swim over your head.

Conversation Topics

- Octopuses live in the ocean! What other fish live in the ocean? Would you like to be an octopus? Why or why not? Would you like to have *eight arms?* What would you do if you had eight arms?

Book Suggestions

- *Good Thing You're Not an Octopus!* by Julie Markes and Maggie Smith
- *Good Night, Octopus* by Caleb Burroughs and Emma Randall

More Activities

- Watch a real octopus swim on YouTube. Look at the way it swims. Do you think it can swim fast or slow? Wiggle your arms like an octopus's tentacles! Would you like to be friends with an octopus? What would you do with an octopus friend?

Songs and Videos

- "The Octopus Song" by Maple Leaf Learning on YouTube
- "Octopus Changes Color and Texture—Eilat" by Dmitry Salnikov on YouTube
- "Octopus for Kids" by Socratica Kids on YouTube

Same and Different Fish

Directions

Circle the fish in each row that look the *same*.

Color Same and Different Fish

Directions

Color the two fish so they look the *same*.

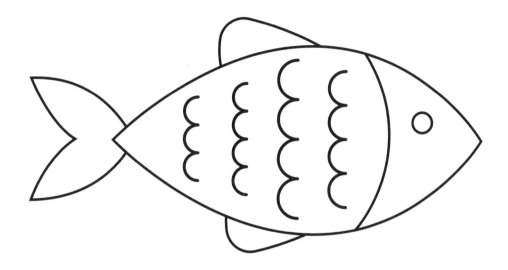

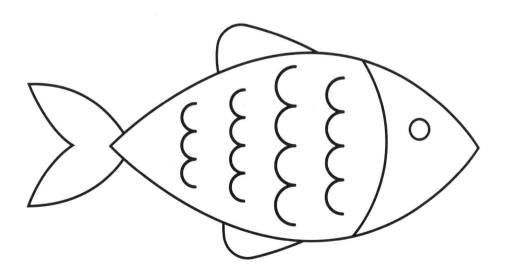

Color the two fish so they look *different*.

Fish Shapes

Directions

There are triangles, circles, and squares on these fish! Can you find them? Color the circles blue, color the triangles green, and color the squares yellow.

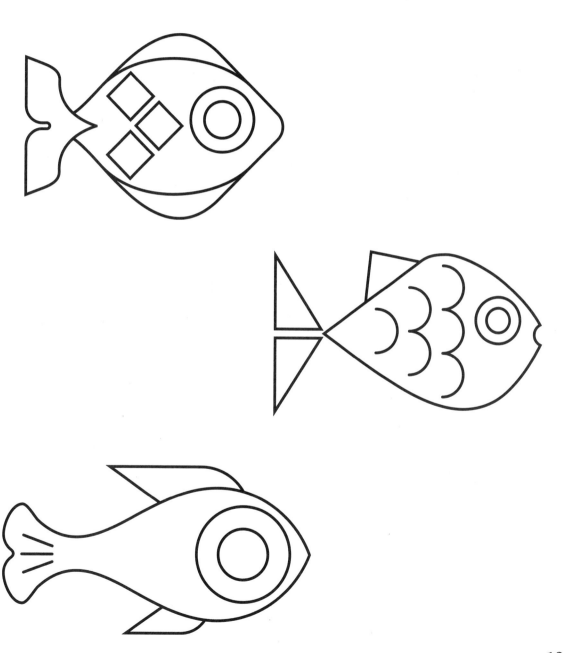

Extension Activities

Parents, here are some extension activities to promote language development with fish play.

Core Vocabulary

- swim
- ocean
- saltwater
- fish
- sand
- square
- circle
- triangle
- green
- yellow
- blue
- same
- different

Following Directions

Work with your child on the following activities:

- Cut out the fish you colored for same and different. Make them "swim" around the house.
- With the fish shapes, practice pointing to the different shapes. For example, ask them to point to a triangle or point to a circle."

Conversation Topics

Look for a video of fish swimming in the ocean or in an aquarium. Talk about what the fish look like.

- Are they big or small?
- Are they blowing bubbles?
- Do you like to swim?
- What is your favorite thing about the water?

Book Suggestions

- *The Rainbow Fish* by Marcus Pfister
- *Way Down Deep in the Deep Blue Sea* by Jan Peck and Valeria Petrone
- *Ten Little Fish* by Audrey Wood and Bruce Wood

More Activities

- With play dough, shape some fish with your child. Make the fish different sizes, and ask your child to identify the big and small fish.
- If you have fish-shaped crackers, take out a handful and practice counting them together.

Songs and Videos

🚂 "Slippery Fish" by Kinder Tunes on YouTube

🚂 "The Goldfish (Let's Go Swimming)" by the Laurie Berkner Band on YouTube

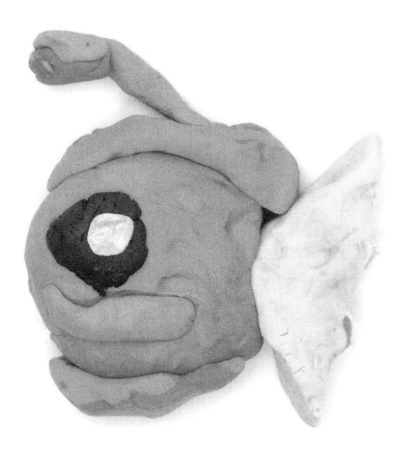

Lion Mask

Roar! Color and cut out the lion mask—don't forget to cut out the eye holes. Hold up the mask and pretend you're a lion. If you want, ask an adult to attach strings so you can tie your mask on.

Feed the Monkey

Directions

The monkey is so hungry! Cut out the monkey on page 141. Ask an adult to help you cut out his mouth! Cut out the big and little bananas below, and practice feeding the monkey. Feed the monkey a *big* banana or a *little* banana. Practice distinguishing between the two. How many bananas did the monkey eat?

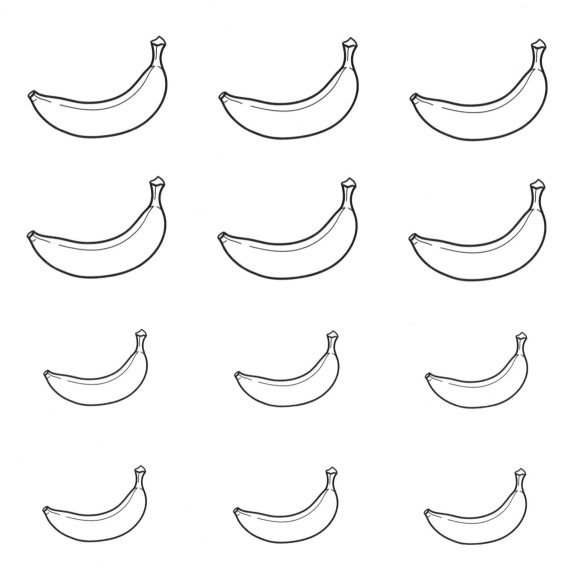

Where Do They Belong?

Directions

Oh no! Animals have escaped the zoo! Some animals fly in the sky, some animals swim in the sea, and some animals roam on the ground. Color the animals below. Then cut them out and glue them to where they belong on page 145.

Act Like an Animal

Animals move in different ways. Color the animals, then do what the animals do!

The elephant STOMPS.

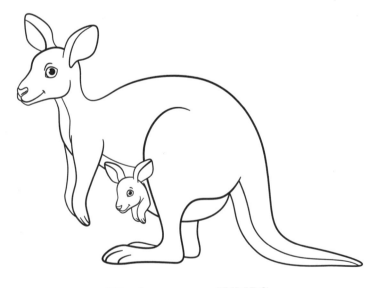

The kangaroo JUMPS.

146

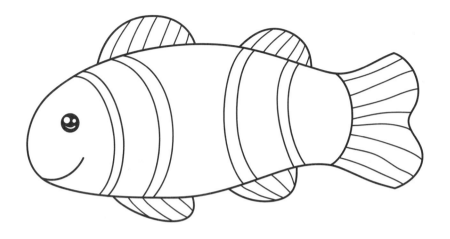

The fish SWIMS.

The monkey SWINGS.

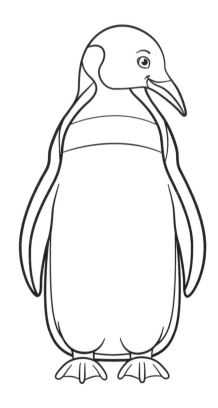

The penguin WADDLES.

Extension Activities

Parents, here are some extension activities to promote language development with zoo animal play.

Core Vocabulary

- zoo
- zoo animals
- lion
- tiger
- bear
- elephant
- roar
- monkey sounds
- growl
- hiss

- big
- little
- fly
- swim
- stomp
- jump
- swing
- waddle
- swim

Following Directions

- Ask your child, "Do you remember how animals move?" Next, have them stomp like an elephant and swim like a fish. Have them try doing the actions fast and slow. Say, "Swim fast like a fish! Now swim slow! What other movements do animals do? Think of your own!"

Conversation Topics

- What's your favorite animal?
- Do you like to go to the zoo?
- What's your favorite part?
- What sound does a ___ make? (Examples: lion, bear, etc.)

Book Suggestions

- *Good Night, Gorilla* by Peggy Rathmann
- *Dear Zoo: A Lift-the-Flap Book* by Rod Campbell
- *Brown Bear, Brown Bear, What Do You See?* by Bill Martin Jr. and Eric Carle
- *From Head to Toe* by Eric Carle

Visit the San Diego Zoo website for kids (https://kids.sandiegozoo.org/) and look through their activities for children. There are coloring pages, crafts, games, and recipes. We like the swinging monkey craft and the memory game. There are also stories available on the website about animals in their zoo. Talk about the different animals you see at the zoo.

Songs and Videos

"Let's Go to the Zoo" by Super Simple Songs on YouTube

"Sesame Street: Murray Goes to the Zoo" by Sesame Street on YouTube

How Do You Feel?

Sometimes you feel happy, and sometimes you feel sad or angry. When you feel happy, your face might look like this: your mouth will go up in a smile. When you feel sad, your face might look like this: your mouth will go down, and you might have tears dripping down your face. When you feel angry, your face might look like this: your mouth will go down, and your eyebrows will point downward.

How are you feeling today?

Extension Activities

Parents, here are some extension activities to promote language development with play around our feelings.

Core Vocabulary

- happy
- sad
- angry
- worried
- hungry
- smile
- frown
- surprised
- scared

Following Directions

- Have your child make a sad face. Make your mouth go down as an example. Ask, "Can you pretend to cry?" Now make a mad face. Say, "Let's make our eyebrows scrunch in a frown." Finally, practice making happy faces. Put on a big smile!

Conversation Topics

- What makes you feel happy? I feel happy when ___ (Examples: when I get a yummy treat, when I get a hug, etc.)
- What makes you feel angry or sad?
- Tell me about a time you felt scared.

Book Suggestions

- *The Color Monster: A Story about Emotions* by Anna Llenas
- *My Friend Is Sad* by Mo Willems
- *Wemberly Worried* by Kevin Henkes

More Activities

- Watch the movie *Inside Out*. Talk about the different emotions and what each one looked like.
- Look through your child's favorite picture books. Can you find any pictures of the characters showing emotion? What do they look like when they're sad? What about when they're angry?
- Get some sidewalk chalk and go outside to draw happy, sad, and mad faces. Remember to talk about what they look like and times you felt all these emotions.

Songs and Videos

- "The Emotions Song" by Sesame Studios on YouTube
- "If You're Happy" by Super Simple Songs on YouTube

Build Your Own Birthday Cake

Directions

It's time to make a yummy birthday cake! Color the cake your favorite flavor. Do you like chocolate or vanilla? Maybe you like strawberry or carrot cake. Color the frosting and enough candles for your cake as well. Cut them out and assemble your cake. Delicious!

Extension Activities

Parents, here are some extension activities to promote language development with birthday play.

Core Vocabulary

- birthday
- cake
- candles
- present
- gift
- party
- balloons
- boxes
- gift wrap
- bows
- ribbon
- slice
- frosting
- layers
- hat

Following Directions

- Ask your child to count the candles on the cake. Ask, "How many are there?" Point to each candle and then the cake.
- Practice spatial directions with the cake by putting the cake *in front* of Mom, or putting the cake *next* to Dad.

Conversation Topics

- When is your birthday? Ask your family when their birthdays are.
- What do you like to do on your birthday?
- Do you like cake? What kind of cake do you like?

Book Suggestions

- *If You Give a Pig a Party* by Laura Numeroff and Felicia Bond
- *Duck & Goose: A Gift for Goose* by Tad Hills
- *The Birthday Box* by Leslie Patricelli
- *When's My Birthday?* by Julie Fogliano and Christian Robinson
- *Happy Birthday, Moon* by Frank Asch

- Have a pretend birthday party for your child's favorite doll or toy. Sing "Happy Birthday" together. Make birthday cards. Make invitations to invite friends to your pretend party. Use play dough to make birthday treats. Decorate with the cake you just colored, and wear your party hats.

- Wrap a present, or pretend to wrap a gift. Use spare wrapping paper or newspaper to wrap a real present or an empty box for pretend. Talk about the shape of the present, what could be inside of the box, and who the present is for.

Songs and Videos

- "Happy Birthday to You Song for Kids" by the Kiboomers on YouTube
- "Baby Shark's Birthday" by Pinkfong! Kids' Songs & Stories on YouTube

CONCLUSION

We hope you've had fun completing our worksheets and extension activities. Sharing enjoyable activities with your child fosters great language development and creates a closer bond between you. Here are some additional suggestions to cultivate your child's language throughout the day:

Follow your child's interests. Children, like adults, are more likely to talk about what they're interested in. When your child demonstrates an interest in a particular topic, expand on it. Look up books, videos, and songs that pertain to that topic or theme. For example, if your child loves trains, spend some time talking about trains. Find train toys and point out if they're going fast or slow, if the train is long or short, and what the train could be carrying. Find child-friendly videos on YouTube of real trains and talk about what you see. For example, "Wow! That train is so big! Where do you think it's going?" You could also find many train-related cartoons or children's movies.

Exploring the world is a great way to stimulate language. Visiting different places allows you to introduce new vocabulary to your child. Point out items of interest and name them. Talk about what the item is used for and perhaps who uses it. Observe the clothing associated with the location. If there are uniforms, talk about what the uniforms look like and why they are used. If certain clothing items are worn (like hiking boots or a hat for sun protection), discuss why they are necessary for that environment.

Explore a range of fun places! Consider taking your child to free public places, such as the library and parks. You can also find ways to expand your child's horizons by simply checking out stores other than the ones you usually frequent. This can include visiting different grocery stores, malls, hardware stores, or other specialty stores. Discuss how these places are the same as and different from the ones you typically go to. Look up what your community may offer. Some fire stations have visiting days for young children, and many cities have free museums.

Take a trip to your local nursery. Point out the unique plants and talk about your favorites. Check out the great outdoors. Beaches, lakes, hiking trails, and other open spaces provide tons of language opportunities. Use your senses: talk about smelling the salty air at the beach, seeing the blue sky, touching the smooth leaf, and hearing the animals or wind in the trees.

For a special treat, consider going to a place like the zoo, an aquarium, a botanical garden, or an amusement park. These experiences lend themselves to a lot of conversation! Be sure to take photographs. Bring them out at a later date to talk about what you remember. Share your experiences with friends or family.

Children learn from repetition, so feel free to repeat their favorite activities. If there is an expansion activity that they loved from the book, or a place they enjoyed visiting, it is okay to do it again. Something like reading the same book over and over again may be tiring to an adult, but it is a great way for children to practice using language in a familiar setting.

Use what's in your environment to inspire language. Buying new toys and games can be fun, but using what you already have access to can provide wonderful language activities. Collect twigs and leaves from outside to make a nest for an imaginary bird or a stuffed animal. Talk about what you've found and what makes a good home for a bird. Create a fort from pillows, couch cushions, and blankets and pretend to camp inside your home. Make microwave s'mores and use flashlights while you talk about what it might be like to camp outside.

Cooking is always a great way to practice language skills. Something simple like making a peanut butter and jelly sandwich can teach following directions and sequencing (such as, "*first* we get out the bread, *then* we spread the peanut butter"). You can target vocabulary words such as sticky, sweet, spread, knife, slice.

Our favorite resources:

- Some of the children's YouTube channels that we particularly like are Super Simple Songs, Patty Shukla Kids, the Learning Station, Sesame Street, and NatGeo Kids. Be sure to preview the videos before watching with your child, just in case there is unexpected questionable content.

- The public library offers a variety of free materials. Local librarians can steer you to books about your child's favorite topics. Libraries also provide a variety of movies and music to explore. Many libraries often host story time or free activities for children.

- Some child-friendly stores such as Lakeshore Learning and craft stores like Joann's offer free activities for children. Check online for free events in your area.

Enjoy your time talking with your child, and have fun learning together!

ACKNOWLEDGMENTS

We would like to thank Bruce Laikko for his support and culinary skills. We couldn't have done it without your fabulous meals to sustain us. We would also like to thank Casie Vogel, Ashten Evans, and the rest of our wonderful team at Ulysses Press for putting in so much work to make our book look good. We'd also like to thank all the amazing creators making inclusive and inspiring work for children, from children's book authors to YouTube contributors.

ABOUT THE AUTHORS

Teresa Laikko is a certified speech-language pathologist who has worked for over thirty years in various settings. She has provided services in schools, private practice, and home health, and has owned her own successful private speech pathology practice. She is a bilingual Spanish-English speaker and has provided services for a variety of populations, including infants, toddlers, school-aged children, and adults. Teresa has worked with clients with autism, apraxia, fluency disorders, intellectual impairments, and articulation and language delays and disorders. She is a member of the American Speech-Language-Hearing Association. Teresa lives in Phoenix, Arizona, with her husband and goofy dog. She's a proud mother of Daniel and Laura Laikko. This is her second book about talking with toddlers.

Laura Laikko is a certified speech-language pathologist who is currently working with special-needs preschool-aged children. Laura has worked with clients with autism, apraxia, fluency disorders, intellectual impairments, and articulation and language delays and disorders. She is a member of the American Speech-Language-Hearing Association. This is her second book about talking with toddlers.